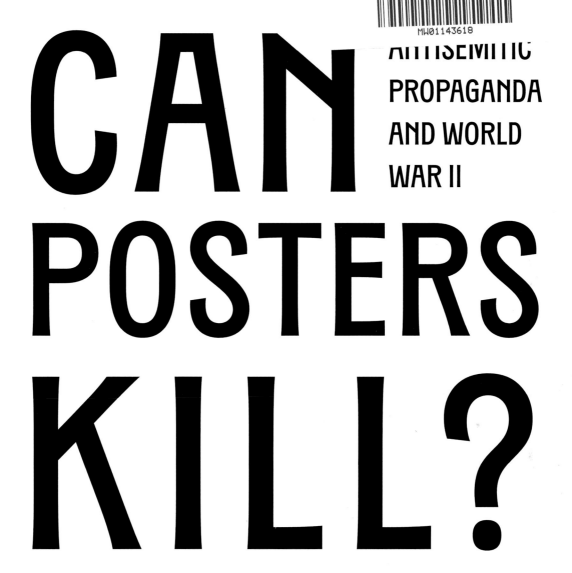

CAN POSTERS KILL?

ANTISEMITIC PROPAGANDA AND WORLD WAR II

JERRY FAIVISH WITH KATHRYN COLE

Second Story Press

Library and Archives Canada Cataloguing in Publication

Title: Can posters kill? : antisemitic propaganda and World War II / Jerry Faivish
with Kathryn Cole.
Names: Faivish, Jerry, author. | Cole, Kathryn, author
Description: Includes bibliographical references and index.
Identifiers: Canadiana (print) 20250156431 | Canadiana (ebook) 20250156555 |
ISBN 9781772604290 (softcover) | ISBN 9781772604306 (EPUB)
Subjects: LCSH: World War, 1939-1945—Posters. | LCSH: World War, 1939-
1945—Propaganda. | LCSH: World War, 1939-1945—Propaganda—Car-
icatures and cartoons. | LCSH: Anti-Jewish propaganda—Germany. |
LCSH: Nazi propaganda. | LCSH: Antisemitism—Germany. | LCSH:
Posters, German. | LCSH: Holocaust, Jewish (1939-1945
Classification: LCC D743.25 .F35 2025 | DDC 940.53022/2—dc23

Edited by Kathryn Cole
Cover design and interior layout by Laura Atherton

All efforts have been made to obtain permissions to reproduce all the posters in
this book from their copyright holders, as listed on page 107.

*Second Story Press gratefully acknowledges the support of the Ontario Arts
Council and the Canada Council for the Arts for our publishing program. We
acknowledge the financial support of the Government of Canada through the
Canada Book Fund.*

Published by
SECOND STORY PRESS
120 Carlton Street, Suite 412
Toronto, ON, M5A 4K2
www.secondstorypress.ca

This book is dedicated to:

My parents, Sam and Lola Faivish, who survived the war and took it upon themselves to move forward and rebuild the Jewish Mesorah the Nazis tried to destroy.

My sister Yona, whose English name translates to dove.

The dove is a symbol of peace that was very dear to my parents.

Yona passed away in 1998.

And to:

Uncle Josek and Auntie Topcza Wolfowicz and their children, Margie and Helen Wolfe, who were my father's closest living relatives and followed a similar pattern of survival, growth, and accomplishment.

While actually more distant relatives, our lives became so intertwined that we called them uncle, aunt, and close cousins.

TABLE OF CONTENTS

PREFACE

I have often been asked what made me decide to collect propaganda posters against Jewish people. There are several reasons. First and foremost, I am a child of two Holocaust survivors, and my life has been influenced by their experiences leading up to and including **World War II** and its aftermath. My family's terrors, you might say, became part of my Jewish heritage and inheritance. The fact that I had very few relatives growing up was another reason. Those missing relatives were my constant reminder of the responsibility we all have to ensure nothing as terrible as the Holocaust happens again—against Jews or *any* group of people.

How easily the figure of six million trips off the tongue. That's how many Jews are estimated to have been murdered by Hitler and his relentless campaign to erase Jews from the world. The loss is so huge that it is hard to comprehend.

Take the time to count from one to one hundred by ones. Counting briskly, this took me about seventy-five seconds. Now, multiply one hundred by ten to get a thousand. If you multiply that thousand by one thousand more, you will get one million. *Six* million Jews were murdered during the **Holocaust**. Even though it's not possible, counting to that number (at the same speed you counted to a hundred) would take 1,250 hours; about fifty-two days and nights without pause, to include every lost person!

Just try to imagine a face and a name for each number. Every one of them was an infant, a child, an adult, or an elder. Imagine your own mother, father, sisters, brothers, aunts, uncles, cousins, and grandparents among them. I don't have to imagine; most of my relatives were in that group. The impact of what happened is clear. Six *million* innocent people became a staggering loss to the world simply because they were Jewish. The collection of propaganda in this book focuses on the Nazis' primary campaign of antisemitism, but we can add millions of non-Jewish victims to the Nazi extermination campaign: prisoners of war, Romani people, people with disabilities, LGBTQ+ people (particularly gay men), ethnic minorities, and many others who the Nazis targeted.

When writing nonfiction books, it's important to talk about the "who, what, why, when, where, and how" of the subject. As for the Holocaust, we know much about to whom, what, why, when, and where it happened. It's that troublesome *how* that has bothered and fascinated others like me over the years. How on earth did people come to hate, participate in, or turn a blind eye to the disappearance of six million people?

This brings me back to my collection of anti-Jewish posters and why I started it. My "aha" moment occurred when I was visiting a relative in Tel Aviv who lived near a major thoroughfare. On one street corner stood a pole plastered with posters advertising products and announcing the coming week's events. None of the images I had seen the previous week were visible; they had all been plastered over with fresh posters touting new products and events. This poster pole, with layer upon layer of current events that reflected ideas and community issues, provided a fabulous but fleeting glimpse of Jewish life in that area. The posters represented a sort-of history designed to attract the viewer's attention and prompt immediate action. Posters, by their very nature, are meant to elicit this kind of response: *Act now, before it's too late.*

These notices for the most part were not meant to offer information or records to future historians or collectors. They were usually not dated. They often contained phrases such as "Attend this Friday" or "Available till January 15." Without context, many could have referred to any month, and most could have been any year. Still, they represented a "current" picture of the times.

Unfortunately, in my travels and searches, I sometimes came across posters that had far more sinister intentions. They had not been put up by local members of the Jewish community but had been produced and distributed by people promoting **antisemitism**— the hatred of Jews.

Will some things never change? I wondered. I realized that— hidden below current notices on similar poles right across

Europe—there could well still be anti-Jewish posters from the Nazi era. They had sent compelling messages calling for people to despise, shun, and even kill Jews. Hitler's poster campaign was huge, calculated, and effective. Through repetition, vivid images, and urgent words, it was designed to promote fear, then disgust, then hatred, and ultimately, mass murder.

To a degree, the posters were part of *how* the killing happened. Hitler used them to say: Act now (against Jews), before it's too late. Standing in front of that pole in Tel Aviv, I decided to collect antisemitic posters that survived World War II as an important part of my overall Jewish poster collection.

For many, these vile images are viewed as taboo and should be destroyed, and I understand that. But I strongly feel they should be shown as a warning so people can recognize and prevent similar campaigns from succeeding again. Even now, the mere mention of these posters often causes severe pain and anxiety to those who suffered through the Holocaust. But some survivors, my parents included, have encouraged me to collect and display them. I truly hope that exposing the posters in this context will help younger generations be better prepared to stem the flow of hatred toward *any* group of "others," whether their difference is religion, race, sexual orientation, or country of origin.

INTRODUCTION

World War II involved much of the globe and was one of the bloodiest periods in history. While the war spanned from 1939–1945, Adolf Hitler's political career began much earlier. After more than a decade leading the National Socialist German Workers Party (Nazi Party for short), one failed **coup**, and nine months spent in prison for treason, Hitler was surprisingly elected as **Chancellor** of Germany in 1933. He wasted very little time passing the **Enabling Act** to make himself a powerful dictator. Given his past actions, a criminal conviction, and his published personal manifesto *Mein Kampf* (*My Struggle*), which clearly laid out his politics, ideology, and plans for Germany, his rise to complete control is hard to fathom.

The war began in 1939 when the Nazis invaded Poland. Nazi Germany went on to invade and occupy over twenty countries before its final defeat in 1945. The key players were the **Allies** (primarily Great Britain, the Soviet Union, and the United States) and the **Axis** (primarily Germany, Italy, and Japan). Allegiances shifted throughout the war, but notably, neither the Soviet Union nor the US joined the fighting until two years in. Italy, originally a part of the Axis, eventually surrendered to the Allies and in turn was invaded by Nazi forces. Nazi Germany surrendered in May of 1945, with Japan following five months later, after the US dropped atomic bombs on Hiroshima and Nagasaki.

How did Hitler convince so many people to follow him in a bloody campaign fuelled by hatred? In the 1930s, Germany was deeply divided with political extremes on both the left and right. Germans were reeling from the **Great Depression** and the economic impacts of their loss in **World War I**. Part of Hitler's strategy involved a comprehensive social and political campaign that started long before 1939 and fed into public fear, anger, and exhaustion. In him lay the promise not only to restore Germany but to exceed its former greatness. Perhaps that promise was so appealing that people ignored any misgivings they had and supported him.

Like social media today, visual communication in the 30s and 40s—from movies to newspapers to paper posters—was clever and interesting, engaging and effective. But under Nazi manipulation, it became deadly.

This book is a collection of some posters from before, during, and after World War II. It shows the visual language of propaganda and hatred. Some posters are overt, others are far more subtle, but all of them contributed to the coordinated mass effort to convince everyone—from children to politicians, organizations to religious institutions—to condone the mass roundup and murder of millions of people whom Hitler claimed were "genetically diseased" and impure. The cover of this book asks the question, Can Posters Kill? Take an analytical approach as you read. By the time you have finished you may well say, "No, posters can't kill, but they can lead people to."

SECTION 1

PRE-WORLD WAR II POSTERS: 1933-1939

Introduction

Posters from 1933 to 1939 generally reflect the work of Hitler's newly formed **Ministry of Propaganda**. The posters blatantly emphasized the long arm of the **Nazi Party**. The status and resources given by the government to promote the Nazi antisemitic agenda became more apparent as Hitler's power increased. In 1928, Hitler appointed Paul Joseph Goebbels, already the district leader of the Nazi Party in Berlin, as the propaganda director for Germany. The ministry of propaganda also had the seal of government approval in places Germany annexed or controlled, such as Austria and Czechoslovakia. Posters were often grouped together in themes or styles: newspaper posters and cartoons, antisemitic caricatures depicting Jews as calculating and greedy, and portrayal of Jews as power-hungry threats to the **Aryan race**. As Goebbels succeeded, his power grew along with Hitler's, and soon he had control of radio, the press, the arts (including literature), stage and film productions, fine art, and even music.

Translation: The Jews have until 10:00 a.m. on Saturday to reflect. Then the struggle commences. The Jews of the world want to destroy Germany! German people resist! Don't buy from Jews.

After the end of World War I, a peace agreement called the **Treaty of Versailles** was enacted. It contained a war guilt clause that set out monetary penalties and other punishments for Germany to pay for its part in the conflict. This caused Germany financial hardship, loss of most of its fighting forces and weaponry, as well as much of its territory, population, and resources. Germans were angry because they felt this was unfair. Moreover, they were disgraced in front of the rest of the world. It was convenient, then, for Hitler to deflect the blame and shame onto Jews and other minorities. By doing so, his popularity skyrocketed, making his rise to power easier.

From a poster pole, very much like the one I saw in Tel Aviv years later, comes a clear warning. This 1933 poster, mild by comparison to those that will follow, announces the coming of the anti-Jewish boycott organized by the Nazis. The clever use of different typefaces grabs the attention of passersby. The message is loud and urgent and warns Jewish people that they are about to face even harder times. It also places Jews, many of whom were successful shopkeepers, at the very center of Germany's difficulties and begins to isolate them from their neighbors by cutting off their income.

We don't even need to see the faces of people reading the poster. Look at their body language. Can you see curiosity, confusion, apprehension, and perhaps even the beginning of dread? The pole on this spring day in Berlin has stopped people in their tracks. Their destinations have become secondary. When they eventually move on, they will have much to think about and discuss. The word will spread. Perhaps some in that poster's audience will begin to make decisions they never dreamed of making.

Although this image is not a poster, it *is* evidence of the very long-standing practice of identifying and isolating Jews from the general population. Antisemitism goes way back to ancient times, but this is a painting from the **Medieval period**. It reflects the laws that were put in place to brand Jews as outsiders. The man on the right is being forced to wear specific clothing that tells others he is a Jew—a person with restricted freedoms. Jewish people were required to wear an identifying badge and hat so they could easily be spotted and prevented from owning land, joining mostly Christian craft guilds, and finding ways to prosper.

The Nazis reintroduced this centuries-old identification policy before and during World War II by making it mandatory for Jews to wear a yellow **Star of David**. Relatively few people who didn't look Jewish and refused to sew the star badge on their clothing managed to avoid the law and escape. For the most part, the traditional identification rules worked effectively—but not in Nazi-occupied Denmark. Most of the Danish Jewish population survived because there, wearing the yellow star was not required, and laws against them were not enforced. They had support from their king, government, and countrymen. There is even a legend that King Christian of Denmark himself wore the Star of David in solidarity with his Jewish subjects, but that is apparently not true. However, in 1943, with his knowledge and the help of Danish citizens, about seven thousand Jews were hidden or spirited away on all types of boats that carried them to safety in neutral Sweden.

Partial Translation: Museum of Horrors (The Freak Show), Number 6

The Traitor

To understand this antisemitic poster, we must go back to France, 1894, when something called the **Dreyfus Affair** began. It caused great division in the country and continued until 1906, when the issue was finally resolved.

Alfred Dreyfus, a captain in the French army, was wrongfully accused of giving French military secrets to the Germans. Because he was Jewish, the people against Dreyfus found it easy to blend the words *traitor* and *Jew* together in an effort to stir up anger against him. Upon his conviction for treason, Dreyfus spent five years of his sentence in a **penal colony** on Devil's Island, aptly named for its terrible conditions.

But Dreyfus supporters remained active. One of them, Lieutenant Colonel Georges Picquart, uncovered the real culprit and presented his evidence to military officials. Perhaps because they wanted to avoid scandal and/or were antisemites, they immediately concealed the evidence and even added more charges against Dreyfus! Opposing newspapers chose sides, but gradually public opinion for Dreyfus improved, as did the demand for justice. He was returned to France, and after more twists and turns, his conviction was overturned. But the affair left France deeply divided, with antisemitism much stronger than before.

This antisemitic poster is the sixth in a series that represents Dreyfus and his supporters as grotesque animals. Here, a hydra, or multi-headed serpent, squirms as it's punctured by a sword declaring it a traitor. In Greek mythology, if a hydra's head was severed from its body, two more grew in its place. This serpent bears Dreyfus's likeness and the inference is clear; the Jews are doubling in power even as we try to stop them. Snakes, age-old symbols of evil, writhe and strike out at all that is good. As you will see later, snakes became a popular tool used by Nazis to promote negative feelings toward Jewish people.

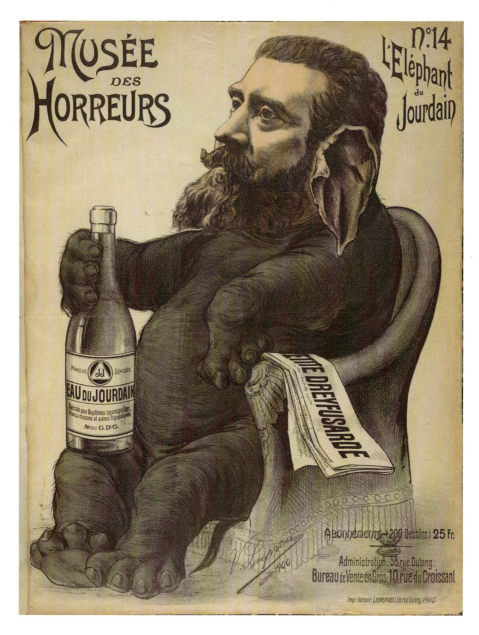

Partial Translation: Museum of Horrors, Number 14

The Elephant From Jordan

This is number fourteen in the *Museum of Horrors* or *Freak Show* series created by an antisemitic artist under the name of V. Lenepveu. He generated these works to protest the government's pardon that set Alfred Dreyfus free. This image shows Jean Jaurès, a man who was initially against Dreyfus but who reversed his stand in the face the growing proof of injustice.

Originally, one hundred and fifty to two hundred such posters were planned, but the French Ministry of the Interior put a stop to them. Only about fifty images were ever printed. They were widely distributed, however, and did much to escalate the hatred and division already within France.

Number 14 shows Jean Jaurès, a brilliant man of complicated **socialist** politics. Here he is literally the elephant in the room. Perhaps his heavy belly and profile inspired the artist to ridicule Jaurès with this particular animal. The elephant holds a bottle of water from the Jordan River, a reference to the claim that Dreyfus's son was baptized in that holy water. The newspaper under the elephant's arm declares him a Dreyfus ally. Although this is certainly grotesque, it is not as violent as many of the other posters in the series. It is meant to undermine Jaurès, who often changed his mind and shifted his political stance. Ironically, one might almost think Jaurès's relaxed attitude and intelligent gaze complement the elephant's reputation for wisdom and power. Jaurès tried unsuccessfully to prevent World War I and to promote reconciliation between France and Germany, but his life was cut short when he was assassinated in 1914 by a young French nationalist.

This brutal antisemitic poster was produced in Austria in 1920 two years after the end of World War I. The **Christian Socialist Party** of Austria generated it before an upcoming national election. It shows a weird and repulsive hybrid creature with the wings and neck of a vulture and the body of a snake. Atop the neck is a caricature of a Jewish man. He wears sidelocks and a **skullcap** and displays his forked tongue, the symbol of a liar. The snake's body has encircled the Austrian eagle and is squeezing the lifeblood from it. The Austrian shield on its chest is almost obscured. Its right claw still clutches the drooping sickle that represents the industrious famers and artisans of the country. His left claw, however, has already dropped the hammer, a symbol of strength and power.

The Christian Socialist Party loudly touted antisemitism in its election campaign at a time when hatred for Jews was on the rise across much of Europe, especially in nearby Germany and France. The party wanted to stop immigrant Jews from entering Austria and to segregate those already there from the rest of society. The Christian Socialist Party won the election on this platform and governed for the following eight years.

Partial Translation: A Farsighted Englishman...

...foresaw the development of the United States thirty-three years ago in 1909, when he published this drawing.

Much earlier, in 1885, the well-known Jewish historian Heinrich Graetz made the following remarkable prediction in London, England: "The Jewish people will one day live in America and will flourish in the land of freedom and equality. A great, powerful Judaism will emerge in the twentieth century."

That is exactly what has happened in the United States. The Jews have achieved their goal and are now the real masters in the USA. They have driven the American people into war in order to extend their power over Europe and the rest of the world. We must defend ourselves against this! We will not lay down our weapons until Judaism and those who support it are defeated and its influence is destroyed.

The power of Judaism is coming to an end!

This poster was first produced and distributed on August 12, 1942, but the illustration in the center of the poster was taken from a 1919 American publication. This biased view shows a "history" of the United States. First, the land is inhabited and controlled by Indigenous peoples. Then **Uncle Sam** arrives, throwing them off the cliff and seizing power, while in the background, a Jew lurks. Next, the Jew comes out of hiding and, in turn, pushes Uncle Sam off the cliff. The final image shows the Jew in complete control of the United States. This image attempted plant fear in the general population by portraying Jews as power-hungry manipulators of world affairs.

The antisemitic rhetoric created by others was repeated by the Nazis during their poster campaign. This poster is from the *Parole der Woche* (*Word of the Week*) series, which was published almost weekly from 1936 until approximately 1943, when a paper shortage caused its demise. The series bombarded people with antisemitic images and context in public places: bus shelters, walls, parks, and poster poles. Wherever people went, the repeated sightings left lasting impressions. Each week, thousands of posters were printed and distributed in Germany and its occupied territories. Posters were the primary medium for the series, but smaller pamphlets, which could be plastered on the back of correspondence, were also produced.

Although this particular poster is very heavy with text, the bold, black headline shouts for attention and causes people to draw nearer. It may have been effective, but this poster isn't typical of the later ones produced by Goebbels's propaganda campaign. They usually displayed short, urgent messages, bright colors, and large central images.

Partial Translation:

Top:

150 Years Ago

I'm Warning You, Gentlemen..!

Bottom:

Did the Great Franklin Warn America in Vain?

"Quotes" from noteworthy sources were used by the Nazis to support their own antisemitism and to demonstrate how the Jewish "problem" was more than a German one. They tried to prove it had, in fact, been of worldwide concern for many years. The use of Benjamin Franklin's name and picture served this purpose admirably. Franklin was one of the most respected American figures in the USA, having helped to write the **Declaration of Independence** and the **United States Constitution**. This propaganda poster from 1939 was also part of the *Word of the Week* series. It shows excerpts from an antisemitic speech falsely attributed to Benjamin Franklin, but this was of no consequence to its creators. The first publication of the speech was on February 3, 1934, in *Liberation*, a paper published by William Dudley Pelley, a Nazi sympathizer and founder of the Silver Shirt Legion of America. This group was aligned with the German American Bund. Both organizations upheld **white supremacist** beliefs, antisemitism, and were Nazi sympathizers. According to the falsified speech, Franklin believed that Jews were totally corrupt and, if left unchecked, would flood the country and overwhelm society.

The speech was quickly debunked as a fraud by the Franklin Institute and others. No matter. Because the speech paralleled their beliefs, it was still widely spread by Nazi leaders through radio, written, and spoken word.

SECTION 2

WORLD WAR II POSTERS: 1939–1945

Introduction

During the war, a much broader reach for propaganda was achieved as countries fell under the control of the Nazi war machine. There are many examples of French, Ukrainian, Russian, Serbian, Dutch, Belgian, Italian, and Hungarian posters. The antisemitic words and images placed emphasis on local issues and widespread dislike of Jews. They insisted that the Nazis were the true victims of Jewish plots, and Jews were, therefore, the enemy. The posters tried to recruit German or Aryan sympathizers and to encourage the war effort. And they were very effective. A false message, when repeated often enough, can become the truth in the minds of people who are frightened, oppressed, and searching for someone to blame for their misfortune during hard times.

Translation: When Jews laugh

The Jews are born criminals. They cannot laugh freely and openly. Their faces are twisted into devilish grins.

This poster was produced in 1937/38 and was an advertisement for the rabidly antisemitic newspaper *Der Sturmer*. It should be noted that although it was aligned with Nazi ideals, the paper was not an official instrument of the Nazi Party. It was a private, money-making publication that promoted hate and the elimination of Jewish people.

Der Sturmer appeared weekly from 1923 to 1945 and by the end of the war, its circulation was well over four hundred and fifty thousand. Julius Streicher, its publisher, blamed Jews for Germany's defeat in World War I, the Great Depression, and basically for all of Germany's hardships after that. In fact, the paper's slogan was, "Jews are our misfortune."

This particular poster focuses on devious Jews gloating while the Aryan (white, blond, blue-eyed) Germans suffer. Because they can't laugh aloud at their plotting, they just smile knowingly. The image warns that supposed friendly and happy expressions are hiding the deceit and secret actions of "two-faced" Jews. Right up to the end of the war, the paper used technique after technique to promote hatred of Jews, a war against Jews, and a campaign to kill Jews and put a final end to their activities.

Partial Translation: We Must Rise Up! ...The Jew is a different race and our enemy.

The Nazis, as part of their propaganda machine, often recycled images used in other countries and at other times to legitimize their hatred and persecution of Jews. One good example is the reprinting in 1943 of a fifty-four-year-old French poster. It was originally produced by A.D. Willette, a candidate in the Paris elections of September 1889. The poster shows the French population, represented by French workers and **Marianne** (the symbol for Liberty and the French Republic) leading the charge against the Jewish enemy. Below her, at the front of the group, a helmeted man holds the severed head of a **golden calf**, an antisemitic symbol. Here, with closed eyes and dripping blood, it is clearly vanquished. The defeated Jews are also represented by a broken **Talmud** at the feet of the now-free French workers. The poster shows that Willette proudly promoted himself as an antisemite and claimed that the Jews were enemies of the French people.

By recycling this poster, the Nazis were holding up long-held "truths" about Jews and implying, "You see? We're not the only ones! Fixing this long-standing problem is for the good of the world."

Due to its origin in earlier times, this poster lacks the finely tuned techniques used by Goebbels. The image is small and busy, making instant recognition from a distance difficult. No bright colors attract attention, and the poster is very text-heavy, requiring the viewer to come up close and have the interest to read all the way to the bottom.

Translation: The Eternal Jew

This poster advertises an anti-Jewish exhibition coordinated by Goebbels and the Ministry of Propaganda. The exhibit was first shown in Munich between November 1937 and January 1938 and was presented in a number of cities. Over four hundred thousand people saw the exhibit. It showed the Jews as **Marxists**, money-lenders, enslavers, and communists, among other things. Jews were shown encompassing all the bad traits of humanity and were basically considered subhuman.

In his own words, Goebbels reveals he knew exactly how to do his work for the Ministry of Propaganda: "The rank and file are usually much more primitive than we imagine. Propaganda must, therefore, always be essentially simple and repetitious. In the long run, only he will achieve basic results in influencing public opinion who is able to reduce problems to the simplest terms and who has the courage to keep forever repeating them in the simplified form, despite the objections of intellectuals."

This promotional poster shows the Jew holding coins, a map of Russia (with the hammer and sickle), and a whip at the ready to punish or control those who resist him. The black and dominant figure against a bright yellow background was designed (as many road signs are today) for high visibility, even from a distance. *The Eternal Jew* was later made into a movie, which was not as well received as films such as *The Rothschilds* or *Jud Süss*. Many people did not see the exhibit but saw the poster promoting it…and got the message.

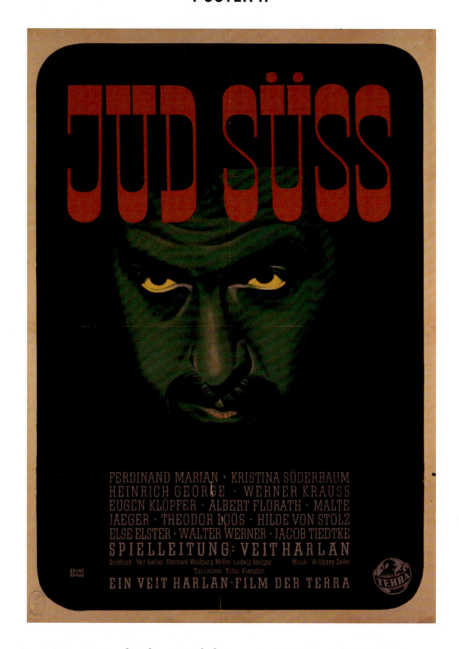

Partial Translation: [The] Jew Süss [...] Screenplay: Veit Harlan, Eberhard Wolfgang Moller Ludwig Metager, Music: Wolfgang Zeller, Sound system: Tobi's sound film

A VEIT HARLAN FILM OF THE TERRA

The movie *Jud Süss* was based on a novel written by the Jewish author, Leon Fruchandler. A British film based on the book was produced in the early 1930s and showed Jews in a positive light. But in the late 1930s, Goebbels "encouraged" an all-star antisemitic version of *Jud Süss*. It was produced by Veit Harlan under the guidance of the Ministry of Propaganda. In this version, the main character, Süss Oppenheimer, coerces and swindles his way through the film until he corrupts the legitimate government and ends up wielding huge power. The movie was extremely antisemitic and became very popular not only for its content, but also for its superior production. In 1940, it ran in about eighty theaters in Munich and Berlin. In the first year alone, twenty million people saw *Jud Süss*. Goebbels also ordered it to be shown to **SS** troops and guards in camps, giving them a sense of justification and furthering their cruel treatment of Jewish prisoners.

Goebbels was thrilled with the movie's success, and because he had the power to control the entertainment industry, he went on to order more such "entertainment." Although the results never measured up to *Jud Süss*, they did form a body of work that I refer to as "Nazis at the Movies."

This widely circulated poster both advertised the movie and solidified people's hatred of Jewry. One doesn't even need to see the film to know Süss's large nose, evil expression, and glowing eyes are meant to spark fear and revulsion toward Jews in all "patriotic citizens."

Harlan was eventually charged with crimes against humanity for his participation in making this movie. He wrote a pamphlet in his own defense declaring he hadn't wanted to make the film, and that Goebbels really was responsible for producing it. Harlan was acquitted. The acquittal was appealed but held up, and Harlan was set free. The vile film has been locked away and is not available for public screenings.

This is a German poster promoting a 1940 antisemitic film about the Rothschild family. It was directed by Erich Waschneck and produced by C.M. Kohn. The Rothschilds were an exceedingly wealthy banking family and had branches throughout Europe that were run by various relatives. Although they had enough money and influence to escape from the Nazis before the war began, they lost much of their wealth, property, and extensive collections, which were seized by the regime. The film, of course, portrayed this family—and Jews in general—very negatively, and the Rothschild name almost became a code word for "the international Jewish banker."

Interestingly enough, the poster does not depict the Rothschilds as unbecoming Jewish caricatures, like those found in other propaganda material. Perhaps that is because real actors portrayed them in the film. Maybe the Rothschilds were familiar enough that the public wouldn't readily recognize them in such unflattering images. What *is* important to note is that the Nazis controlled media and cultural events. Virtually nothing could be released without government approval. The seal on the lower right-hand side of the poster shows government approval of the advertisement and movie for general distribution. The film was one of three produced and promoted by Goebbels and the Ministry of Propaganda.

Translation: Tuberculosis, Syphilis, Cancer

are curable....

We must put an end to the greatest of scourges:

the JEW!

This notice was used in wartime France. It equates Jews with diseases and spreaders of disease. Here, a doctor or scientist is looking through a microscope only to find a vicious Jewish disease devouring healthy tissue. Jews were often characterized as sexual deviants and were blamed for spreading tuberculosis, syphilis, and cancer. They were also accused of seducing and raping non-Jewish women. The clear message here is that it is "good medicine" to end the plagues created and spread by these people, and to avoid, or even eliminate them. It's a chilling message because it can quickly turn into "kill or be killed."

Translation: Protect Yourself From Typhus

Avoid Jews

On the same theme as the previous French poster, this Polish one shows an old Jewish man wearing a skullcap. Obviously miserable and unhealthy himself, he huddles in the dark underworld, crawling with huge, insect-like germs, which represent the deadly typhus disease. The central figure is flanked on the left by a skull (none too subtly standing in for Death) and a Jewish star on the right. This implies that the Jew spreads typhus, and moreover, this deadly illness can be released and controlled by him at will. In Nazi literature, the Jews *purposely* spread typhus to the general non-Jewish population. And again, the viewer's natural reaction to this "information" can easily sway from avoiding Jews, to getting rid of them altogether. By promoting this kind of fear, the Nazis met less resistance from the public as people who were once friends and neighbors were persecuted for being "dangerous enemies." It is, after all, much easier to justify killing in self-defense as a necessity, rather than murder. This poster was produced in Poland under Nazi occupation in 1941.

Partial Translation: ...this Jewish dream of ruling the world is vanquished under the blows of rising nationalism!

Here we see a Jew crowned by a *Magen David* (Star of David). He hovers menacingly over the globe, spinning a web from his index finger. This reinforces the Nazi-supported notion that Jews are power-hungry and backed by secret cabals or conspirators. The image also refers to the widely touted belief that Jews could make the globe spin on its axis according to their wishes.

To send a quick message, this antisemitic poster relies on a powerful image to make its impact. The brief text is clearly visible and reinforced by the bold, red words at the bottom. Even from a distance, people could grasp the meaning and feel the fear and urgency it was meant to foster. This, and the following nine posters, were created to attract people to an anti-Masonic, anti-Jewish exhibit in the Nazi-occupied territory of Serbia. It was frequently alleged that Freemasons were a front for Jews and were tools of the Jewish conspiracy to rule the world. The exhibit lasted approximately three months and ran in Belgrade from October 1941 to January 1942. Sixty thousand copies of each poster were printed weekly and flooded public places where they could not be ignored. The exhibit alone was attended by eighty thousand people.

Who were the Freemasons, and why were the Nazis against them? The origins of this fraternal (all male) group are uncertain, but some records go back as far as 1646. Masonry is thought to be centered around customs and legends of stone masons who built castles and cathedrals in medieval times. The Masonic symbol shows an open compass and a set square (a right angle), both architectural and geometric tools used by stone masons. The Freemasons exist worldwide today and are known not only to support each other, but to contribute to many charities and worthy causes. Their meetings are closed, and that led the Nazis to believe the Freemasons were conspiring against Hitler's regime. Propaganda against Freemasons went along with hatred of Jews and other minority groups. It is estimated the Nazis killed up to two hundred thousand Freemasons while they were in power.

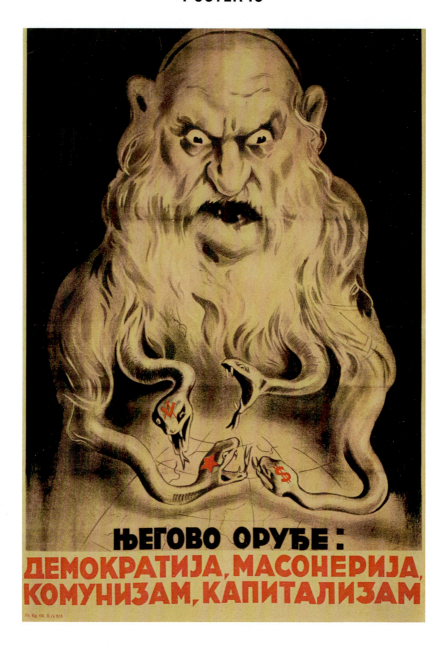

Translation: His Weapons:
Democracy, Masonry, Communism, Capitalism

In 1933, Hermann Goring (also spelled Göring), acting as **Reichstag** President, stated, "In National Socialist Germany, there is no place for Freemasonry." Thus, the masons were considered undesirable and were banned in Germany in 1934. They became targets of Nazi oppression along with Jews, Black people, the **Roma**, and members of the LGBTQ+ community. Lumping them in with Jews served to strengthen the negative public opinion of anyone who wasn't "pure" Aryan.

Here, a wicked Jew hovers over the world like a four-headed serpent. He is portrayed as an evil assassin with poisonous snakes writhing in his beard. From biblical times, the snake has represented sneakiness and evil because of its role in convincing Adam and Eve to sin in the Garden of Eden. This image tries to demonstrate that Jews are as venomous as the fanged creatures they conceal within; they will stop at nothing to contaminate and corrupt their enemies.

The man is shown in the worst possible light. Wearing a Jewish skullcap, he is toothless, long-nosed, and predatory. Almost decaying before our eyes, he is the stuff of nightmares. Three visible symbols on the serpent heads are the Star of David (representing Jews), the dollar sign (representing control over world economy), and the compass and square (symbol of the Freemasons).

The theme and written message are the same in the following poster.

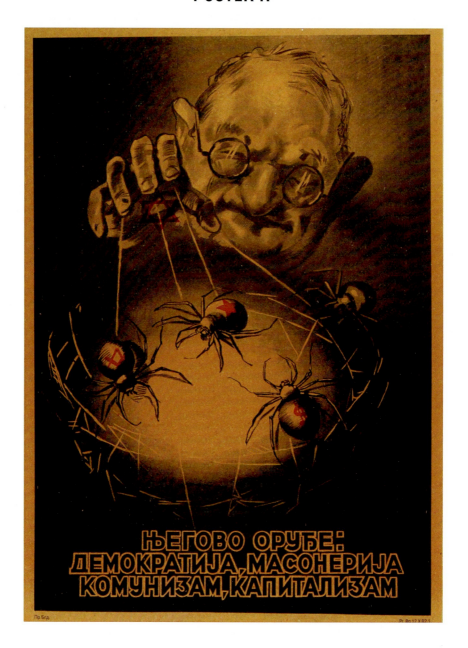

Translation: His Weapons:

Democracy, Masonry, Communism, Capitalism

This was also one of the posters from occupied Serbia that was part of the **Grand Anti-Masonic Exhibition** in Belgrade. This image repeats the so-called Jewish plot to dominate the entire globe. Although the color scheme is more muted than those in many of the other posters, the message is just as clear and alarming. A powerful and focused Jew hovers over the world and happily releases his weapons—spiders to weave webs of entrapment. The creatures are marked with symbols: a dollar sign, a communist star, a Freemason's tool. The Star of David is in the man's palm. This time the figure is not as grotesque as usual, but the reflections in his glasses obscure a secret intent that cannot easily be read in his eyes. The choice of spiders to do his bidding is brilliant. The creatures have long been associated with witchcraft and sinister entities. Spiders also seem to revolt and startle many people. Their webs are sticky enough to catch unsuspecting prey, and their eight long legs enable them to appear quickly and then scurry to safety. The bites of some can be poisonous, but in reality, very few humans get sick or die from them. Spiders only bite people in self-defense, and most of the time, humans aren't even aware they have been bitten. Still, spiders, or pictures of them, tend to incite genuine fear and strong, negative reactions.

Translation: Ninety-eight percent of the finances in the United States is in Jewish hands

"Nothing is easier than leading people on a leash. I just put up dazzling campaign posters and they jump right through it." —Joseph Goebbels

Harping on the repeated and now-familiar theme, this image plays into the antisemitic view that Jews have control of all economies worldwide. This particular image is of the Jewish American, Henry Morgenthau Jr., who was appointed Secretary of the Treasury in 1934. The picture shows a small Uncle Sam, bowing, and dutifully pouring gold coins into Morgenthau's lap.

As US President Roosevelt's Secretary of the Treasury, Morgenthau was instrumental in setting up a system of marketing **War Bonds**. The War Bond program raised billions of dollars toward the cost of America's eventual entry into World War ll. This, along with his Jewishness, made him a major enemy of Hitler's Nazi regime.

Again, constant repetition of such images hammered home the notion that Jews and other minorities were not to be trusted as neighbors, leaders, or even citizens. The notion eventually became the "truth" in the minds of many, making their hatred and persecution not only acceptable, but patriotic.

This is also a Serbian poster from the Belgrade exhibition.

Partial Translation: Ninety-seven percent of the American Press is in Jewish hands

In a similar light, this Serbian poster claims that Jews control virtually all of the media in the United States. It specifically refers to *The New York Times*, a well-known and important American newspaper owned by the Jewish Ochs Sulzberger family. The image shows a Jew bursting through the pages of *The New York Times,* thus "proving" the false claim that Jewish ownership of the media enabled Jews to control worldwide events and the reporting of them. This long-standing, groundless notion was repeated long and loud and influenced public opinion. Surely, if Jews controlled the world's finances and kept their hold on power out of the news, they were to be feared, hated, *and* stopped. This Nazi propaganda was especially ironic since Hitler's regime had, by this time, seized Jewish assets and censored the free press at home.

Another quote from Joseph Goebbels indicates why he was a good choice as Hitler's propaganda director: "It would not be impossible to prove with sufficient repetition and psychological understanding of the people concerned that a square is, in fact, a circle. What, after all, are a *square* and a *circle*? They are mere words, and words can be molded until they cloak ideas in disguise."

Goebbels was a master at what he was doing. This technique of repeating lies until they become "truths" is still used today by some political figures attempting to gain support for their own agendas.

Translation: Here's the culprit!

This image refers to the fact—or the *alleged* fact—that Jews control all major governments and are behind the schemes put forward by capitalists, communists, and the British, all of whom were Jews—at least, according to the Nazis. The poster shows a well-dressed, sneaky individual lurking behind translucent curtains made from the flags of England, the United States, and the Soviet Union (1922–1991). The man is obviously wealthy and Jewish as his clothing, golden chain, and Star of David show. With his exaggerated facial features and calculating expression, he is supposedly the supreme power behind the enemies of Nazi Germany. The poster is Serbian, but other versions of it exist in various European languages.

Again, representing the Jewish people as foes of the Aryan master race and the cause of everyone's troubles, promoted public support for Hitler's anti-Jewish policies. With some posters having a weekly circulation of sixty thousand, the campaign was a form of brainwashing. Remember, by this time, the Nazis had control of the press, radio, and other publications. With no internet or computers in common public use, posters were an important source of information.

Translation: His Weapons:

Democracy, Masonry, Communism, Capitalism

Up until now, most of the images we've seen show the Jew in a sinister but fairly passive way. He has been sneakily gaining wealth and power behind the scenes. But here, the vicious Jew is callously demonstrating that he will stop at nothing in order to dominate his enemies. Again, the accusation is that the Jew uses democracy, Masonry, **communism**, and **capitalism** as tools to help him control world affairs.

There is an old saying, Nero fiddles while Rome burns. Nero was a very unpopular and cruel emperor in Ancient Roman times. He was hated for many reasons, one was his persecution of Christians. Legend has it that during the great fire of Rome, he did nothing (or fiddled) while disaster ensued.

This poster is clearly a warning to the general population. If they stand by doing nothing about the Jews, they are headed for death and destruction. Note that the sky behind the fiddler is not daytime blue or nighttime black. It is red, the color of danger, anger, and alarm. Spectators view this image from a low perspective, putting them in the position of the skeletons and under the power of the enemy. The message is, "Act now. It's kill or be killed." The red, italic text reinforces the urgency to do something before it's too late.

Ironically, if the head of this fiddler were replaced by Hitler's, this picture would depict exactly what happened to the Jewish people under Nazi rule.

Translation: Jewish Balance

The poster depicts a large, powerful Jew controlling the balance of the world by standing astride the center of a teeter-totter on top of the globe. Again, his position and size indicate world domination. Sitting on the ends of the seesaw are US President Roosevelt with his crutch and Prime Minister Winston Churchill of the United Kingdom. Both men are portrayed as overweight and weak. Unable to touch the ground or move unless the board is tipped by the domineering central figure, they look questioningly at him as if asking how long they will be stuck in this position. The expression and stance of the Jew seems to say they will be up in the air and under his power for a very long time.

Yellow can symbolize contrasting emotions. It can mean happiness and sunshine when used in positive ways. But used negatively, as it is here, it symbolizes greed, jealousy, cowardice, and warning. Yellow is also highly visible from a distance, making it an excellent choice here. With only two words, the image speaks volumes and sends the message that the "Jewish problem" is worldwide and needs to be stopped.

Translation: You don't know yet...beware!

The poster depicts a vicious-looking Jew caught in the act of murdering various European and US politicians. His immense size, and thus his huge power, enables him to tighten the rope around their necks with relative ease. As if the message wasn't clear enough, a small Magen David is shown in yellow on his *kippah* (skullcap).

This antisemitic propaganda poster was also part of the Grand Anti-Masonic Exhibition in Nazi-occupied Belgrade, which approximately eighty thousand people viewed. Multiple images of violence committed by Jews and messages such as this one must have made the attendees' blood run cold. Since alternate media was scarce and mostly under Nazi control, these anti-Jewish messages went, for the most part, unchallenged. There was very little to persuade anyone that all of this "evil" Jewish activity wasn't actually happening.

Translation: Who will overtake? No one! Because the Jew controls the balance.... Visit the ANTI-MASONIC EXHIBITION and you will see for yourself.

This is yet another variation of the Jews controlling the balance of the world. This time, the balance is literally held by the Jew manipulating the scales. His influence is enormous because he can control current events and alliances between countries, changing the balance of power. Sometimes, the anti-Masonic, anti-Jewish poster exhibit showed the Jews being opposite things simultaneously. This time, he is communist (represented by Stalin on one dish) and capitalist (represented by American and British gold on the other).

Communism and capitalism are opposing systems. In communism, production from factories, land, and natural resources are publicly owned. What society needs is considered more important than individual freedom, and all citizens are supposed to be equal. In capitalism, property, factories, and resources are privately owned, and individual freedom and autonomy is emphasized. This creates a competitive society where some people grow wealthier than others.

Why did the Nazis show Jews as having opposing identities? Because it helped convince people how untrustworthy and changeable they were. If your enemy is unpredictable and coming from every direction, you are in greater danger. In this way, Nazis convinced people that the sly Jews were working solely in their own interests by using whatever means suited them.

Right now, the scales are equally balanced, and only the Jew knows who he will favor to come out on top. His expression and hands seem to indicate he is enjoying his power. Despite his satisfied smile, the lighting from below reinforces the impression this huge sinister figure is to be feared.

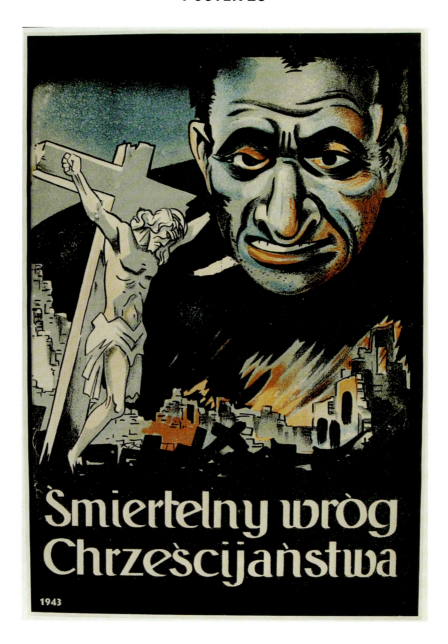

Translation: The mortal enemy of Christianity

This time, the poster image shows a devilish Jew overlooking Christ on a crucifix while a Polish village is destroyed by fire. This poster was an advertisement for a 1943 pamphlet titled *The Mortal Enemy of Christianity*. Shrouded in black and with dramatic lighting, the Jew's exaggerated features reveal a wicked, self-satisfied sneer.

The Jews have long been accused of killing Christ, who himself was Jewish. This is not true. Jesus was sentenced to death and crucified by the Roman rulers of the time. This false accusation goes back two thousand years and is one basis for the long-held, religious hatred of Jews.

The poster image was based on a 1937 illustration that was previously published in *Der Sturmer* (or *Der Stürmer*), a weekly antisemitic German tabloid. It is from Nazi-occupied Poland. The Nazis were promoting the notion that not only were Jews responsible for Christ's death, but now they were burning cities and villages throughout Poland. Nazi accusations against the Jewish population systematically increased over time. If Jews were controlling the world's politics and wealth, spreading diseases at will, and destroying Christian land and homes, what else were people supposed to do but fight back…and annihilate them! This poster was produced in 1943, when the Nazis were under severe pressure from the Allies and Russia and were beginning to realize that they might lose the war.

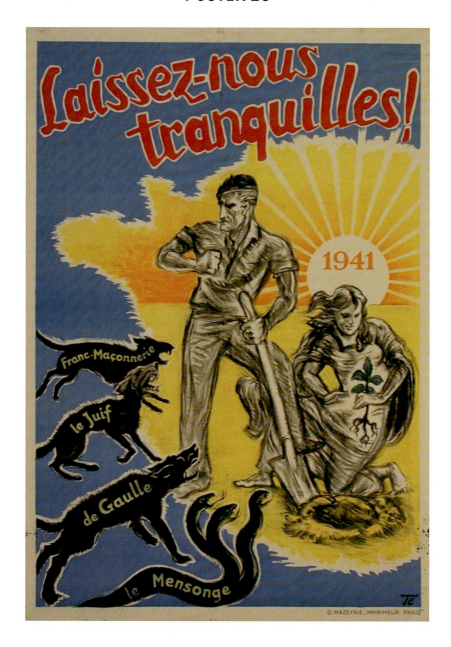

Partial Translation: Leave us in peace!

A young French couple (representing their country) tries to work the land and plant new trees while being hounded by three menacing wolves. They are identified as French Freemasons, the Jews, and the exiled French government led by **Charles de Gaulle**. The wolves are accompanied and supported by a three-headed snake named *le Mensonge* ("the lie"). This poster was produced in France in 1941. It speaks loudly of the falsely touted "Jewish conspiracy" to gain territory and power for themselves and prevent the rebuilding of nations ravaged by war. Living conditions in France at this time were harsh. Much of the country was under Nazi occupation. Food was rationed, and fuel, coal, and clothing were scarce while the winters were cold. War raged as French Jews were persecuted and deported to Nazi concentration camps. In such conditions, fear and exhaustion were familiar to French citizens. No wonder posters such as this one were produced. The Nazis needed to deflect anger and blame away from themselves so they could proceed with their plan with as little resistance as possible.

Translation: The Jewish Plot

Against Europe!

This French poster shows the devil Jew, hovering in darkness and observing the uneasy alliance between Britain and Russia. John Bull, a fictional symbol of the British people, is on the left, and Stalin—fierce, with blood on his free hand—is on the right. Their arms stretch across Europe in a gesture of partnership, while the Jew oversees and controls the action on both sides of the conflict. Once again, he is depicted as an unattractive and unsavory character. He looks fairly assured and at peace with the control he is exerting below. Observers are meant to see this as a Jewish plot against all of Europe. In stark imagery, the outline of Europe is made up of small white dots encompassing a huge landmass. Separate countries no longer exist. Far from being a Jewish plot against Europe, this illustrates Hitler and his Nazi Party's campaign to claim ownership of all this territory for Germany.

Why would the partnership between the Soviet Union and Great Britain—along with her ally the United States—be so uneasy? Because the two powerful democracies had long been rivals of the USSR (Union of Soviet Socialist Republics). Moreover, they were angered and unsettled when, in 1939, Stalin, signed a pact with Nazi Germany that allowed the Soviet invasion of five European countries, including Poland. But in 1941, Germany betrayed Stalin and broke that agreement by invading the Soviet Union! Stalin, whose name means Man of Steel, quickly did an about-face and joined the Allies. This marked a significant turning point in the war. Nazi Germany now had powerful foes to the east, west, and in North America. Uneasy as the new partnership was, the **Big Three** as they came to be known, saw the advantage in joining forces for as long as it took to defeat Hitler's Nazis.

Partial Translation:

THE JEW—YOUR ETERNAL ENEMY!

Who brought blood, tears, and hunger to your country? Jews!

Who supported the executioner Stalin? Jews!

Who abducted and raped your wives and daughters? Jews!

Who squeezed the last blood out of you? Jews!

Who scolded capitalists the loudest, while being the biggest money grabber? Jews!

Who ordered the destruction of your houses by Stalin's will? Jews!

Who tortured millions of people to death in the cellars of the ***NKVD**? Jews!

Who is to blame for the war? Jews!

Who sent millions of people into forced labor? Jews!

Who ordered the destruction of your food stocks at the will of Stalin? Jews!

Bottom:

Stalin and the Jews are a gang of criminals!

*Bold added to mark the glossary term.

Even though it is written in Ukrainian, this poster was published in 1941, probably in Poland, but was intended for the Ukrainian people. The poster merges the Jews with Stalin, the ruthless dictator who held complete power in Soviet Russia until 1953. It lists various accusations of Jewish misdeeds. By linking the Jewish people with Stalin, the message inspires fear and causes hatred. The image shows a despicable, sly Jewish figure with a big nose and *payos* (sidelocks) posed in the middle of a Star of David. The poster casts blame on Jews and claims they are basically responsible for everything bad. See the translation for some examples of the terrible things they supposedly did. The self-satisfied expression of the central character suggests he is benefitting from his behavior. Of course, because the general public was isolated from news of the outside world, there was no way to dispute or doubt this "information." In fact, Stalin had already aligned with Nazi Germany and had eliminated Jews from high government positions. He went on to persecute Jews more widely.

Translation: The Worker and Soldier Unite for Socialism

This is a Belgian poster, printed around 1941, after the Nazi occupation. It attempts to show solidarity for **socialism** between the Belgian workers and Nazi German soldiers. As a recruiting poster, it targets the male population of Belgium and its important port city of Antwerp.

It's easy to see that the Belgian worker and the Nazi soldier have their target on the run. Their enemy has a Jewish face with a large nose and wicked expression. He is the largest figure and represents the United States as he is wearing stars and stripes on his vest and trousers. He is, also wearing a Union Jack on his top hat and a hammer and sickle on his suit lapel. This indicates how the three major enemies of Nazi Germany (Great Britain, the United States, and Russia or the Big Three) are acting together. The briefcase the man is fleeing with represents capitalist bankers.

It is interesting to note that while that image is not subtle, nothing is left to chance. Look at the little finger of the "enemy's" hand. It sports a Magen David to drive home the message that, in fact, the banker is Jewish. As was often the case, the Jew was made to represent all bad things, even if they were contradictory. Here, the Jew is the ally of communism and socialism, and yet, he is the banker who also represents capitalism.

Translation: Italian "allies" divide the spoils while the Jew awaits his time.

This Italian poster shows Hitler's enemies around a dining table shaped like a Jewish star. The table represents the Nazi propaganda view of the Jewish conspiracy to control world affairs. Various countries (Finland, Lithuania, Poland, Turkey, Greece, Bulgaria, Estonia, Romania) are being served on plates as the Allies and Russia divide the spoils of war between themselves. All this is happening under the watchful eyes of two Jews who wait patiently to take over. The first Jew is holding a *menorah*, an ancient symbol of Judaism, and a dagger. The second Jew leans on a book, *The Protocols of the Elders of Zion*. The earliest version of this book was published in Russia in 1903. It claims and promotes the falsehood that a secret group of Jewish elders held meetings and recorded "protocols" or methods by which they could attain and retain global dominance. Though this group never existed, the book is being held up by the second Jew as "proof" of his desire to assume power. The long-nosed, bearded fellow is also holding a smoking grenade. The message is stark: Our enemies will gobble us up, and the violent Jews will manipulate everything.

Translation: The **Waffen-SS** Takes Command

*Bold added to mark the glossary term.

In Belgium, this Nazi propaganda poster showed the SS symbol crushing its Jewish **Bolshevik** foe. The use of strong yet simple images in vivid color is striking. The SS symbol, backed by the outline of a soldier, is killing its adversary. But the small details are what reveal the two hated Nazi enemies. The Magen David (Jewish star) and the communist (Russian) star both hang from a golden chain around the neck of the dying enemy. The final outcome of Jewish and communist domination is represented by the skull and skeleton. Communists were often linked with Jews and were just as often portrayed as one and the same. Frequently, the enemy was one entity with opposing characteristics.

This was a recruitment poster aimed at young Belgian volunteers. The SS symbol dominates the picture and the faceless shadow of a new recruit is meant to appeal to the viewer. The message? Join us, and together we will vanquish the enemy.

This forceful image requires no text at all. The hostile communist Jew, with fists at the ready, eagerly challenges all comers. He stands in front of the New York skyline and the Statue of Liberty, showing his ultimate ambition to maintain control of the world's major powers, first and foremost, the United States. From the look of his bruised, red knuckles, he has already engaged many who tried to stop him. The star just below his left hand is not a Jewish star, it is the symbol of Russian Bolshevism. This links the antisemitic theme that Jews are responsible for the rise of communism in Russia. There was no historic proof of this, but it suited the Nazis to say otherwise, and was constantly put forward to convince doubters were in danger from the entire Jewish race. Here, looking up from a low angle, the viewer is made to feel intimidated and small while establishing direct eye contact with the huge, large-nosed Jewish caricature welcoming a fight. The poster was produced in Nazi-occupied Italy around 1943.

CAN POSTERS KILL?

This World War II poster was published by the United States War Department in 1942 and specifically mentions the massacre in Lidice, Czechoslovakia (now Czech Republic). It was where the Nazis shot (or sent to concentration camps) the entire population of the village.

As the war went on, the Allies placed very little focus on Nazi brutality. This may have been because they didn't have a full grasp of everything happening under Hitler's regime until the liberation of camps and occupied territories. But this American poster does highlight one particularly dramatic example of cruelty. The image shows a hooded victim of the attack on Lidice. Tense, with cuffed hands, he awaits his fate. He is anonymous, faceless—almost as if he never existed—mirroring the complete elimination of his village. The Nazi evil is highlighted by a telegraph, which curtly announces the fate of the village and its inhabitants. The well-known artist Ben Shahn created this and other anti-Nazi posters as part of a campaign financed by the US government. The purpose was to bring sharp attention to the mindset and deeds of Hitler's Nazis for all the world to see.

After the war, a number of posters were printed by the Allies documenting the atrocities committed by the Nazis. Many photographic images were taken by liberators and third parties, but some were taken by the Nazis themselves. Shockingly, meticulous records were kept by the Nazis to preserve their "accomplishments."

As the torture and killings continued throughout the war, they gave rise to inventive ways of inflicting extreme suffering on the "subhuman" victims. Even as Nazi success faded, there was vicious treatment toward Jews and even more efficient mass killings. Severe psychological and physical evil was inflicted in front of prisoners, and so a great many survivors lived the rest of their lives carrying horrific images with them. Their trauma was often passed along to their descendants for generations to come.

SECTION 3

POST–WORLD WAR II POSTERS: 1945

Introduction

After 1945, posters were much fewer in number. Most were related to the **Nuremberg Trials**. The trials were held to convict the Nazis for war crimes they committed during the war. Materials produced by the Nazis leading up to and during the war were introduced as evidence against captured criminals. During the war, photographic evidence of Nazi crimes was not widely distributed and were not used as motivation for murder. Generally, it was intended that there should be shock and revulsion upon seeing the images. However, photographs were more common after the war because they were used as evidence in war crime trials, or they were released as parts of documentaries and newsreels.

As General Eisenhower said, "I never dreamed that such cruelty, bestiality, and savagery could really exist in this world.... I made the visit (to Buchenwald) deliberately, in order to be in a position to give first-hand evidence of these things if ever, in the future, there develops a tendency to charge these allegations merely to 'propaganda'."

Hitler and Goebbels were never captured or tried at Nuremberg. Both committed suicide when Germany lost the war.

This Soviet Union's Ministry of Defense poster was created after the end of the war. It shows a huge Russian flag overshadowing the German *Reichstag* (parliament) building. Here, the statement is clear and boastful, as if Russia is claiming sole responsibility for defeating Hitler's regime. Although the Soviets were certainly not alone in the win and entered the war late, they do have some boasting rights. Their retaliation against Germany for Hitler's betrayal of Stalin and the invasion of their country marked a dramatic turning point in the war. With Soviet power added to that of the other Allies, it was only a matter of time before the Nazis went down in defeat. V-E (Victory in Europe) Day was celebrated on May 8 by the rest of Europe, but because of a time zone difference, the Soviets celebrated on May 9.

The Soviet flag plays another role in this poster. Its dagger-sharp staff has impaled cartoonish figures of Hitler and Goebbels along with other Nazi officers. The way they are depicted almost makes them seem like comical fools in their ruin. This vengeful poster is one-upmanship taken to new heights. The solid blocks of black, yellow, and red make this prideful poster highly visible.

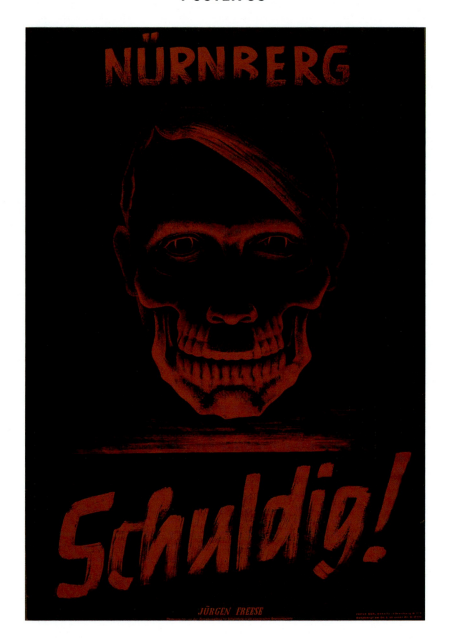

Translation: NUREMBERG

Guilty!

With the fighting over, the Allies held several military trials in Nuremberg, Germany, to bring the remaining Nazi officers to justice. If found guilty, they would be punished as war criminals for atrocities and invasions committed under Hitler's regime. The trials lasted eleven months, starting in November 1945. Some convicted defendants were given life terms, others were sentenced to death, and a few were found not guilty. Many others were *not* held accountable for their actions because they escaped to various parts of the world, including the United States and Canada. Over the years, "Nazi hunters" found some in hiding or under assumed identities. Others were never found. They would now be in their nineties, so the effort to bring them to justice is all but over.

In 1946, *after* the Nuremberg Trials, the Allies printed this poster, which mirrored the general opinion of how the Nazis participated and conducted themselves during the war. The black background, representing a dark time, is highlighted by a bloodred skull. The skull is Adolf Hitler's. The mustache and slanted forelock give him away, as his penetrating eyes bring a chilling sense of living evil to the viewer. The blood spilled by the Nazis is alluded to in Hitler's expression of rage and obsession, even from beyond the grave. During his last living moments, he instructed those he was about to leave behind: "We've got to kill the Jews." The man consumed by hate died with it. Unfortunately, hate did not die with him.

At the war's end, it was felt that most Germans *willingly* took part in the action. This postwar picture is accompanied by the word *Schuldig*, which reflected the Allied sentiment against Germany as a whole: Guilty! With a relentless propaganda machine that often pumped out sixty thousand images a week, we should stop and ask how we might have reacted ourselves. If the propaganda wasn't always believable, it *was* always terrifying. To resist Hitler's laws meant capture and likely death. Even so, many non-Jewish citizens took heroic risks to hide families, take in Jewish children, and transport people to safety.

The Jew, the Enemy

The image combines the Big Three into one sinister portrait of a Jew. The drawing was published in 1944 as the Allies advanced on Germany.

The Jew and the Cemetery

The caption states, "Where Jews live, nations must die. Where nations live, Jews must die."

The Devil and the Servant of God

Perhaps some people have now learned that one can never convert the devil.

While often mocked because of his extreme views, Julius Streicher, who published *Der Sturmer*, had tremendous influence over much of the German population. Depicting the Jews as a source of evil and a symbol of everything that could go wrong, he promoted the Nazi version of hate against the Jew with images such as these.

Streicher eagerly joined the emerging Nazi Party in advance of the war. Before becoming a publisher, he was an elementary school teacher, so he knew how to build and communicate a message. His paper, from beginning to end, was full of nasty stereotypes of Jews committing every hateful sin imaginable. During the war years, *Der Sturmer*'s circulation increased dramatically, generating great wealth for its creator.

Again, *Der Sturmer* was *not* an official organ of the Nazi Party. But by promoting Hitler's **Final Solution**, it strengthened the existing animosity toward Jews and incited readers to comply with, and participate in, the murders that followed. The images that Streicher repeatedly circulated were so inflammatory that he was eventually held criminally liable for publishing them before and during the war.

Streicher was one of twenty-four senior Nazis tried at Nuremberg. He was found guilty of crimes against humanity and sentenced to die. Immediately before he was hanged, Streicher shouted, "*Heil Hitler! The Bolsheviks will hang you all next. Jewish holiday! Jewish holiday, 1946! Now it goes to God.*" This refers to the Jewish holiday **Purim**. Clearly, Julius Streicher carried his hatred of Jews right to the end.

CONCLUSION

The aftermath of World War II left many countries in shambles scrambling to repair, rebuild, and repatriate. Redrawn boundaries and financial hardship, not to mention the loss of so many people, didn't make the job easy. Estimates vary, making it hard to put an exact number on the casualties of WWII, but fifty million is an accepted *conservative* figure. The war created refugees and displaced persons who had great difficulty finding welcoming countries in which to start new lives. Grudges didn't just disappear when the war ended, and some of that animosity has carried right through to the present day.

With the US bombing Hiroshima and Nagasaki in 1945, the war abruptly ended. Much was learned about "modern warfare" and the staggering consequences of using atomic weapons, especially on civilian populations. For a short while, the United States was the only major power to possess such weapons and the American government made very good use of that fact: No one dared to antagonize a power willing unleash such devastation.

Russia raced to develop its own atomic weapons, and four years later, they had them. The **Cold War**, a contest of nerves between communist and democratic countries, was in full swing. Although nine countries now possess atomic weapons, they have never again been used in warfare, but we are forever changed by that possibility.

Also in 1945, the **United Nations** (UN) was formed when fifty-one countries signed its charter. The chief intent of its initial gathering in San Francisco was to devise a mutually agreed upon international policy to safeguard the equality of all people and to maintain peace by diplomatic means. The UN, now with headquarters in New York City, currently has ninety-three member states. True to its original mandate, it also supports humanitarian aid and maintains peacekeeping forces. Founding members included Canada, the United Kingdom, the United States, Russia, Australia, and China. Interestingly, Japan did not join until December of 1956, but it is now an active, productive participant. Each member state, large or small, has equal voting rights.

Through all of this, propaganda has remained a constant factor in promoting discord and outright lies. Antisemitism is, sadly, on the rise again. But propaganda is no longer confined to movies, literature, music, and posters. With events happening in real time on TV and the internet inside our homes (and pockets), and with the dawning of artificial intelligence, also come the fastest and most widespread methods of sending messages, both true and untrue. We live in complicated times, and it is more important than ever to think carefully about what "facts" politicians and radicals want us to believe. Are there hidden agendas behind convincing words?

If hateful propaganda from the past has any use at all, it may be to teach us how campaigns of hatred should not have been used in the first place and must *never* be repeated. That is my hope and sole reason for sharing my collection. While unsettling world events swirl around us, remember that even in the face of evil, most human beings have the ability to be kind, to accept change, right wrongs, and improve the planet. And so do you. If you ever feel overwhelmed by global challenges, try narrowing your focus. Remember how small kindnesses make a huge difference. Be good to one another. Instead of rejecting it, marvel at the beauty in people of all races, religions, cultures, and genders. They can enrich our lives if we allow them to. In a shrinking world, there is no longer a place for fear of the "other."

AFTERWORD

As mentioned in the preface, my parents were survivors of the Holocaust. My mother was in various ghettos, work camps, concentration camps, and at extermination sites such as Auschwitz. My father was jailed early in the war simply for being Jewish and engaging in his family business. Later, he was put on a train cattle car headed for the gas chambers. Seizing a rare chance to escape, he jumped from the train and avoided the imminent claws of the Nazi death machine. My father spent much of the remainder of the war in hiding. When the fighting ended, he crisscrossed Europe, making ends meet, until he ended up in a **displaced persons (DP) camp**—Bergen-Belsen.

During the Nazi regime, my father lost his parents and his eight siblings. My mother only had one brother and one sister survive out of a family of ten. The impact of this loss is hard to imagine. Years later, when I was in grade five or six in Canada, I took an IQ test, which partly examined family relationships. Since most of us were children of Holocaust survivors, we came from nuclear families, our extended families having been wiped out during the war. At the end of the test, many of us were bewildered because we couldn't understand family connections. The originators of the test thought they were writing culturally neutral questions. Obviously, they had never met members of Holocaust-survivor families who were not exposed to, and didn't comprehend, grandparents, cousins, aunts, and uncles.

In retelling my parents' life-and-death experiences, my parents emphasized several things. They told me never to ignore that evil exists in the world. Yet, notwithstanding the horrific things that happened to them and their families as a result of evil, both of my parents cautioned me to remember all of the good things that people did, even under the most trying circumstances.

For example, my father was hidden by a non-Jewish (gentile) family on a farm in Poland, at great risk to their personal safety. Almost every day they told my father they were afraid, and he would have to leave the next morning. Yet, day after day, they gave him one more day. That was true heroism on the part of my father's protectors.

My mother toiled in various work and concentration camps, usually in the kitchens. Numerous Nazi officers showed her and her coworkers great kindness and saved them several times by ignoring infractions. An example of such kindness was allowing my mother to take a nap—a capital offense—during some of her shifts and warning her of danger when the SS (Hitler's elite corps of Nazi soldiers) was approaching. They also let my mother live when she was caught serving more food than was allowed to fellow prisoners. When confronted by this infraction, my mother said, "These are my brothers and sisters. Wouldn't you give more food to your starving brothers and sisters?" Surprisingly, the Nazis let the practice continue, and my mother and her teenaged coworkers saved Jewish lives, one spoonful at a time.

These kindnesses helped my parents survive and gave them a framework for what happened, along with a partial answer to the ultimate question: How was it that they, among so many others, lived?

Those kind acts were echoed by many citizens across Germany and the occupied countries of Europe. Not everyone went along with the Nazis and their propaganda. Countless heroes stood up for what was right, even giving up their own lives to rescue the persecuted. At enormous risk, a large underground movement helped people escape. The **Kindertransport** moved about ten thousand children out of Hitler's reach. Gentiles claimed some Jews were their own visiting relatives, hiding them in plain sight. These selfless acts proved goodness was still alive. After so many years, generations of Germans who were yet to be born have paid a heavy price for the beliefs of the Nazi regime. They have lived with resentment and shame for the events that began in their country. They have tried to face and atone for this dark time in history. They too, have needed to heal.

After the war, my parents met in Bergen-Belsen, the DP camp where they married and started a family. My older sister was born there in 1949. She was given the Hebrew name Tova Beracha, which translates to "good and a blessing." In English, her name was Yona, which represented a dove. To my parents, she brought hope and optimism and a reason to strive for a brighter future. The hope was that they would rebuild Jewish institutions, organizations, and communities that had been lost or destroyed. They also had hope in creating their own Jewish family to continue their traditions.

In 1952, my parents immigrated to Canada. In 1953, I was born in Montreal. For my parents, the question of how to deal with recurring hate, and what could be done about it, was more than philosophical. It became a guideline for how to live their lives and what to pass on to their children. The lessons they taught us are still applicable and valuable today:

- Be proud of who you are and embrace your faith and culture. The aim of the "Final Solution" was to annihilate Jews *and* to destroy Judaism.
- Respect your fellow human beings and treat them well.
- Recognize and eliminate hate and evil as much as possible.
- Do not tolerate examples of racism and stereotyping.
- Do not ignore such examples in the hope they will just go away.
- Stand up for what is right and seize opportunities to do good.
- Don't focus only on yourself but consider others as well.
- Do not engage in racism or stereotyping to lift your own self-esteem.
- Watch your words. Recognize the power and effect they have.

In rabbinic terms, the sages have described hateful language and images as follows: The power of evil speech is like a bag of feathers, dispersed in the wind, that is almost impossible to collect or correct.

Holocaust survivors who overcame the attempt to annihilate the entire Jewish nation scored the ultimate victory. Jews who kept their lives, faith, and pride rose above the efforts of the Nazi regime. They are evidence that Hitler and his followers failed in their mission. Survival and success, not further hatred, are the sweetest forms of victory.

In preparing for this book, I went to a friend's mother who was in her nineties and a Holocaust survivor. Over the years she spoke publicly about the Holocaust and tried to engage others to be actively involved in Holocaust studies. I asked her if I could show her some posters from my collection to see if she remembered any from her youth. She was abhorred by the suggestion. She told me the very thought of having to look at those images made her sick. She simply could not do it. But to my surprise, she then said I should show, explain, and exhibit the posters to as many young people as possible. That way, they could learn what happened, not so very long ago, and prevent its repetition.

I urge you to learn from the past, to apply those lessons going forward, and safeguard against evil. With our constant exposure to social media, question if what you see and hear is true. Does it make sense? Is it what *you* believe or is it what someone *wants* you to believe? Is it good information or bad? Only you have the power and right to make decisions for yourself. In that spirit, I would like to pass the torch of remembrance and prevention to you readers. May you be good and steadfast doves who bring blessings and hope to the future.

SELECTED TIMELINE

January 30, 1933
Adolf Hitler is appointed as German chancellor.

March 14, 1933
The Reich Ministry of Public Enlightenment and Propaganda was created by Hitler and led by Joseph Goebbels, with the intention of shaping German public opinion and behavior.

March 22, 1933
The first concentration camp was established outside the town of Dachau for political prisoners and Jews. It became the prototype for future concentration camps.

March 23, 1933
The Enabling Act was passed, allowing the Reich government to pass new laws without the consent of Germany's parliament. This laid the foundation for Hitler's dictatorship.

November 9–10, 1938
Nazi leaders, including members of the Hitler Youth, carried out a wave of organized **pogroms**. The violent rioters destroyed hundreds of Jewish-owned businesses, homes, and synagogues, and rounded up tens of thousands of Jews to be deported to concentration camps. This became known as ***Kristallnacht***, the "Night of Broken Glass," and was the first time Nazi officials made mass arrests of Jews for no other reason than their being Jewish.

September 15, 1935
The Nuremberg race laws were passed, prioritizing German citizens by Nazi-imposed "superior Aryan race" standards and revoking German citizenship from Jews and other minorities.

August 23, 1939
The Nazi-Soviet Nonaggression Pact was signed between Nazi Germany and the Soviet Union, an agreement not to attack each other for ten years, and included a secret plan to invade and divide Poland between the two countries.

September 1, 1939
Nazi Germany invaded Poland, marking the beginning of World War II.

September 3, 1939
Great Britain and France declared war on Germany.

September 17, 1939
The Soviet Union invaded eastern Poland.

September 27, 1940
The Tripartite Pact was signed in Berlin, solidifying an alliance between Germany, Italy, and Japan, and formalizing the Axis powers.

June 22, 1941
Nazi Germany violated the Nazi-Soviet Nonaggression Pact and invaded the Soviet Union. Soon after, killing units began the mass murder of Soviet Jews.

December 7, 1941
Japan bombed Pearl Harbor. The next day, the United States declared war on Japan, officially entering World War II.

December 11, 1941
Hitler and the United States declared war on each other.

January 1, 1942
Twenty-six countries signed what later became known as the Declaration of the United Nations, promising not to negotiate a separate peace with any countries within the Axis. The following day, a further twenty-two countries signed the declaration. At this point, the "Big Three" (the United Kingdom, the United States, and the Soviet Union) were all allied against the Axis powers.

January 20, 1942
The Wannsee Conference confirmed and finalized the policies and continuing implementation of the "Final Solution," the plan for the mass murder of all Jews in Germany and Nazi-occupied Europe.

September 8, 1943
Italy surrendered unconditionally to the Allies. Nazi forces subsequently invaded Northern Italy.

June 6, 1944
The Allies invaded western Europe, beginning in Normandy, France. All of northern France was liberated by the end of August.

March 7, 1945
US troops crossed the Rhine River into Germany.

April 16, 1945
The Soviets encircled Berlin, their final offensive attack.

April 30, 1945
Hitler died by suicide.

May 1, 1945
Joseph Goebbels, the minister of propaganda, died by suicide.

May 7–8, 1945
Germany signed an unconditional surrender to the Allies.

April 6 and 9, 1945
The United States dropped atomic bombs on Hiroshima and Nagasaki, Japan.

August 8, 1945
The London Agreement is signed, establishing the International Military Tribunal, which was composed of judges from the United States, the United Kingdom, France, and the Soviet Union to conduct a series of trials against war criminals.

September 2, 1945
Japan formally surrendered, officially ending World War II.

October 6, 1945
Leading Nazi officials were indicted for their war crimes.

October 1, 1946
The verdicts for the Nuremberg Trials were announced during the International Military Tribunal, sentencing twelve Nazi officials to death for crimes committed during the Nazi regime. Many key Nazi leaders, including Adolf Hitler and Joseph Goebbels, were never tried for their war crimes as they had had committed suicide or were in hiding.

GLOSSARY

Allies: A military coalition of nations that fought together against the Axis powers (led by Nazi-occupied Germany) in WWII. Principally led by the United Kingdom, the United States, the Soviet Union, and China.

antisemitism: The prejudice, hostility, and discrimination against Jewish people.

Aryan race: A term incorrectly attributed to a "master race" by Hitler and the Nazis but that does not exist. This pseudo race was characterized as, typically, people who are white-skinned, blue-eyed, and blond.

Axis: A military coalition of nations that opposed the Allies and that was led by Nazi-occupied Germany, Italy, and Japan in the Second World War.

the Big Three: The primary leaders of the Allies; the United Kingdom, the Soviet Union, and the United States.

Bolshevik: A member of the extremist wing of the Russian Social-Democratic Workers' Party, which was led by Vladimir Lenin and characterized by Marxist values.

capitalism/capitalist: A system of economics where individuals own and control production and the items used to make goods and services; a capitalist is someone who prescribes to capitalism.

coup: Short for *coup d'état*; a violent overtaking of a current government, usually by the country's own military force.

chancellor: A term for the head of government in some European countries.

Charles de Gaulle: A French general who led the Free French Forces against the Nazis in World War II.

the Cold War: Waged from 1945–1989, it was an intense political and ideological rivalry between the Soviet Union and the western world, particularly the United States, involving threats, propaganda, and a nuclear stalemate.

communism/communist: A system of politics and economics where important resources, such as farms, power plants, and factories, are owned by the public, with income divided equally to all people. An example of a communist country was the Soviet Union; a communist is someone who prescribes to communism.

Christian Socialist Party: A religious and political party in Austria that combined Christianity and socialism, was founded in 1889 by virulent antisemites, and promoted antisemitism leading up to the start of World War II.

Declaration of Independence: The United States of America's founding document of principles and ideals.

displaced persons (DP) camp: Temporary, postwar communal living quarters established by the Allies for Jewish refugees in Germany and Austria.

the Dreyfus Affair: The biggest scandal in France in 1894, when Jewish officer Alfred Dreyfus was wrongly accused of providing secret information to the Germans about the French army. Alfred Dreyfus was imprisoned and was only proven innocent twelve years later. The Dreyfus Affair divided the French population, and many of the people who accused Dreyfus of being a spy were antisemitic.

Enabling Act: A law that allowed Adolf Hitler to dictate new laws and rules without needing the approval of the parliament (Reichstag).

Final Solution: The Nazi's premeditated plan for the mass murder of all Jews in Germany and Nazi-occupied Europe.

golden calf: A statue of a calf made by melting gold that was worshipped by the Israelites. It is believed that worshipping the golden calf was a sin against God as a form of apostasy.

Grand Anti-Masonic Exhibition: An antisemitic exhibition paid for by the Nazis that opened in Belgrade, Serbia, during Nazi occupation in 1941.

the Great Depression: The worst economic global crisis, which took place in the 1930s. Starting from the US and spanning across the world, the Great Depression caused severe unemployment and poverty worldwide for an entire decade.

Holocaust: The systematic, state-sponsored persecution and murder of millions of European people, especially six million Jews, by Hitler, Nazi Germany, and its allies during the Second World War.

Kindertransport: Meaning "children's transport," was a series of rescue efforts during 1938–1940, where children under the age of seventeen were allowed to enter Great Britain as refugees. About ten thousand children, the vast majority being Jewish, were safely sent to Great Britain on kindertransports.

Kristallnacht: Translated as "The Night of Broken Glass," the countrywide pogroms of November 9–10, 1938, in towns and cities throughout Germany and annexed Austria. Nazi leaders and Hitler Youth destroyed hundreds of Jewish-owned businesses, homes, and synagogues, and rounded up tens of thousands of Jews to be deported to concentration camps. This was the first time Nazi officials made mass arrests of Jews for no other reason than their being Jewish.

Marianne: A symbolic figure of a woman wearing a Phrygian cap (liberty cap) that represents the French Republic. Marianne is a symbol of freedom and equality and has been used since the French Revolution.

Marxism/Marxist: The political, economic, and social principles advocated by Karl Marx, including the labor theory of value (the amount of labor required for a good or service determines its worth). It analyzes the impact of the ruling class on workers, leading to uneven distribution of wealth and privileges; a Marxist is someone who prescribes to Marxism.

Medieval period: Or Middle Ages; a period of time in Europe after the classical era and before the modern era, between the fifth and fifteenth centuries.

Ministry of Propaganda: A department of government that controls newspapers, books, art, films, music, etc. In Nazi Germany, one of the Ministry of Propaganda's primary goals was to spread antisemitic ideas and beliefs to the populace.

Nazi Party: The fascist and autocratic (unchecked power) political party led by Adolf Hitler that controlled Germany from 1933–1945.

NKVD: The feared Soviet secret police agency responsible for internal security and the labor prison camps.

Nuremberg Trials: International war crime trials conducted by the Allied forces after the end of World War II, persecuting and convicting Nazi war criminals guilty of crimes against humanity for their actions during the war. These military tribunals took place in Nuremberg, Germany, from November 1945–October 1946.

penal colony: A settlement for prisoners that were exiled from their countries.

pogrom: An organized attack on a specific ethnic group, particularly Jews in Russia or Eastern Europe in the late nineteenth and early twentieth centuries, and later in Nazi Germany.

Purim: A holiday that marks the salvation of the Jewish people from an ancient death decree made in the fifth century BCE.

Roma: An Indo-Aryan ethnic group. Like the Jews, they were persecuted and murdered by the Nazis.

socialism/socialist: A social and economic policy that calls for public rather than private ownership or control of property and natural resources; a socialist is someone who prescribes to socialism.

skullcap: Or kippah; a domed, brimless hat worn by Jewish men as a symbol of Jewish identity.

the SS (Schutzstaffel): Originally established as Hitler's personal guard, they were an elite combat branch of the Nazi Party that carried out security duties, often without legal restraint.

Star of David: Or Magen David; a star with six points and a symbol of Judaism.

Talmud: A compilation of ancient Jewish teachings and is the central text of Rabbinic Judaism.

Third Reich: Meaning the "third empire," it was the Nazi regime from 1933–1945 named by Adolf Hitler to refer to Nazi Germany and its occupied territories.

Treaty of Versailles: A peace treaty that ended World War I. The treaty was signed by countries that fought against the German Empire, declaring that Germany had started the war and demanded the country pay money and give up land among other rules, as a form of reparations. The Treaty of Versailles resulted in a major economic downfall for Germany after WWI.

Uncle Sam: A symbolic figure of an old, white man with a white beard, top hat, and clothes in the color of the American flag (red, white, and blue). Uncle Sam is used to represent the United States as a government and country.

the United Nations (UN): An organization, founded after WWII, of many countries around the globe that work together to discuss world problems and find solutions with the goal of maintaining peace.

United States Constitution: The supreme law of the United States of America that sets the framework of the country's government.

Waffen-SS: The military branch of the SS that was a major part of Nazi Germany's military campaigns in WWII.

War Bonds: A country's way of borrowing money from its people to pay for military and other wartime expenses.

white supremacist: A racist person who believes that the white race is inherently better than all other races and that, therefore, white people should have control in all its forms (social, political, economic, etc.) over people of other races.

World War I (WWI): Also known as the First World War or Great War; one of the deadliest wars in world history that was mostly fought in Europe from 1914–1918, between the Allied Powers (the United Kingdom, Russia, France, Japan, Italy, and the United States) and the Central Powers (Germany, Austria-Hungary, Bulgaria, and the Ottoman Empire).

World War II (WWII): Also known as the Second World War; mostly fought in Europe and Asia from 1939–1945, between the Allied Powers (the United Kingdom, the Soviet Union, France, China, and the United States) and the Axis Powers (Germany, Italy, and Japan). Many catastrophic and deadly events happened in WWII, including the Holocaust and the atomic bombings by the United States in Japan. WWII has the largest number of war deaths recorded in history.

ACKNOWLEDGMENTS

Writing this book has been a lifelong dream—an opportunity to use the posters in my collection to educate others about propaganda and antisemitism. I am honored to thank the many people who helped bring this book to print.

Over the years, various Holocaust survivors and survivor organizations encouraged me to display my posters and sponsored numerous presentations. I am grateful to the teachers and school administrators who invited me to present to their students and explore the impact these posters had on them. Additionally, I appreciate the historians, educators, government officials, and poster dealers who helped me locate and acquire anti-Jewish posters that survived World War II.

The team at Second Story Press has been incredibly supportive and committed to this project. A special thank-you to my cousin, Margie Wolfe, and her dedicated team—Laura Atherton, Jordan Ryder, Emma Rodgers, Phuong Truong, Michaela Stephen, April Masongsong, and Luckshika Rajaratnam.

I am especially grateful to Kathryn Cole, whose insight and collaboration helped bring clarity to my thoughts and played a vital role in bringing this book to life.

I would also like to thank my poster team—Caline Schneider, Marnie Halpern, Myriam Brenner, and Rene Goldman—who have worked diligently to catalog my collection. A special note of gratitude to Rene for her assistance with this book and my personal affairs.

My daughter, Tamara, has provided invaluable help with many of the technical aspects of this book.

To my wife, Miriam, and my children—Tamara and Avraham, Sharona and Naftali, Ronit and Aaron, and Meir—you have long tolerated the spread of my posters throughout our home. Thank you for your unwavering support and appreciation of my work in preserving Jewish posters.

POSTER CREDITS

Page 14 - Yad Vashem
Page 16 - Public Domain
Page 18 - Public Domain
Page 20 - Public Domain
Page 22 - United States Holocaust Memorial Museum
Page 24 - From the personal collection of the author
Page 26 - From the personal collection of the author
Page 30 - From the personal collection of the author
Page 32 - From the personal collection of the author
Page 34 - United States Holocaust Memorial Museum
Page 36 - bpk Bildagentur/Deutsches Historisches Museum/ Rehak, Bruno/Art Resource, NY
Page 38 - From the personal collection of the author
Page 40 - United States Holocaust Memorial Museum
Page 42 - United States Holocaust Memorial Museum
Page 44 - From the personal collection of the author
Page 46 - From the personal collection of the author
Page 48 - United States Holocaust Memorial Museum
Page 50 - From the personal collection of the author
Page 52 - From the personal collection of the author
Page 54 - From the personal collection of the author
Page 56 - From the personal collection of the author
Page 58 - From the personal collection of the author
Page 60 - From the personal collection of the author
Page 62 - From the personal collection of the author
Page 64 - United States Holocaust Memorial Museum
Page 66 - United States Holocaust Memorial Museum
Page 68 - United States Holocaust Memorial Museum
Page 70 - From the personal collection of the author